DISCARD

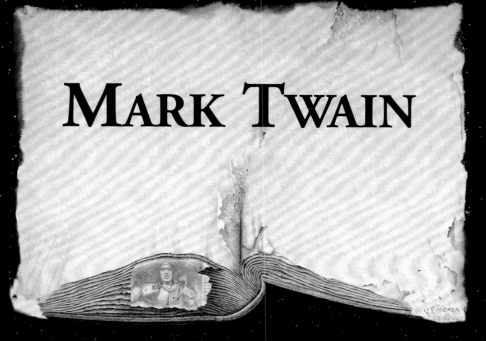

English text copyright
© 2003 Mason Crest Publishers, Inc.
All rights reserved.

Illustrations copyright
© 2001 Andrea Di Gennaro
Published in association with
Grimm Press Ltd., Taiwan

1 3 5 7 9 8 6 4 2

Library of Congress Cataloging-
in-Publication Data

On file at the Library of Congress

ISBN 957-745-414-3

Great Names
MARK TWAIN

Forbush Memorial Library
118 MAIN STREET P.O. BOX 468
WESTMINSTER, MA 01473-0468

Mason Crest Publishers
Philadelphia

ANDREA
DI
GENNARO

On a cold winter's night in 1835, Halley's Comet blazed across sky, as it did every 75 years. In small house in a village in Missouri, the wail of a newborn baby shattered the night. He was the family's fifth child. They called him Samuel Langhorne Clemens.

The tiny baby was premature, and his mother was afraid he wouldn't live through the night. She prayed to God to let him live, and in the midst of her prayers, she saw a star shoot across the sky. "It's a sign from God," she thought. "Somehow this shooting star is linked to my baby."

"I was born the 30th of November, 1835," wrote Clemens, "in the nearly invisible village of Florida, Monroe County, Missouri. The village contained a hundred people and I increased the population by one percent. It is more than many of the best men in history could have done for a town. . . . There is no record of a person doing as much—not even Shakespeare."

As though fulfilling the sign of his birth, Samuel was always on the move, shooting from one place to the next. Adventure seemed to flow through his veins. He never worried, nor did he know the meaning of fear. Exploring was as natural to him as eating, and

ANDREA
DI
GENNARO

nothing could stop him when his curiosity was aroused. Anything that was forbidden was irresistible to him. If he thought something would be fun, he simply did it. Fun was all that mattered to him.

Samuel loved exploring caves. In the pitch dark, he searched for human skeletons, bats, mysterious passageways, and pirate treasure. He was convinced that clever pirates had hidden their gold in the limestone caves of Missouri. One of his favorite tricks was to stuff a bat in his pocket and take it home to frighten his mother.

"I was born excited."

Because Samuel was also born premature, he was a sickly child. Measles, pneumonia, and constant colds almost killed him. He survived these crises, but his active imagination created new terrors, filling his dreams with massacres, hangings, robberies, and other horrifying scenes.

His nightmares were very realistic and frightening. He began to sleepwalk. His sleepwalking always followed the same path. He walked to the barn, climbed up on the white horse, and sat there, motionless.

Samuel's active imagination also gave him a reputation as a liar. He once told his friends and brothers that when he was a week old, he walked to the fireplace, that at nine days old, he had pretended to be stabbed by his diaper pin, and that when he was six weeks old, he had shared a glass of whiskey with his grandfather.

ANDREA DI GENNARO

His tall tales left his listeners speechless. Samuel had another storytelling talent. He would retell stories he had heard, making himself the main character, so that it sounded as if everything in the story had actually happened to him. But he wasn't really a liar. He told these stories to impress people, not to deceive them.

"A man's private thoughts can never be a lie; what he thinks, is to him the truth, always."

When Samuel was four years old, his family moved to Hannibal, Missouri, on the banks of the Mississippi River. Shortly after this move, Samuel heard the whistle of an approaching steamboat and saw the towns-people as they streamed toward the port to greet the boat. Little Samuel eagerly joined the crowd, running as fast as his legs would carry him. "How big is it?" he wondered. "Bigger than a house?" From the moment he saw his first steamboat, he had only one wish: to be a river boatman when he grew up.

"Once a day, a cheap, gaudy packet arrived upward from St. Louis, and another downward from Keokuk. Before these events the day was glorious with expectancy; after them, the day was a dead and empty thing."

Samuel's head was full of dreams, and his curiosity led him into all sorts of adventures. Danger made him itch with excitement. As soon as no one was looking, he would disappear, like a puff of smoke. One day, he

nearly drowned after jumping in the river. His mother couldn't keep up with his misadventures, so she sent him to school when he was four and a half.

In the 1830s, the children of Hannibal attended school for less than one dollar a week. At school, they studied reading, spelling, etiquette, the Bible, and arithmetic. On his first day, Samuel was punished for not standing up when his teacher called his name. He was ordered to go outside and find a suitable stick with which he could be beaten. Samuel looked around and finally chose a rotten tree branch. When he gave it to the teacher, the teacher said nothing. Instead, he ordered another student to fetch a proper stick. This was just the first of many punishments, as Samuel made more trouble than all the other students put together.

Samuel hated rules, and he hated lessons. At school, time seemed to move more slowly than a snail. From Monday to Friday, Samuel dreamed of Saturday. Most of the time, he sat at his desk daydreaming. Sometimes, he livened things up by letting a snake loose in the classroom or putting a frog on a classmate's head.

After a while, Samuel began to plot ways to avoid going to school. In the morning, he would examine his body for spots, bumps, or bruises. If, by some chance, he found something, he would lie on the bed, groaning loudly, bringing his anxious parents

ANDREA
DI
GENNARO

to his side. In fact, Samuel had outgrown being a sickly child. He only pretended to be sick, especially on fine days, when the sun shone brightly and a gentle breeze was blowing. School seemed terrible compared to what the river offered. There were fish to catch, caves to explore, and water fights.

"My childhood was filled with warm and wonderful memories. None of these happy memories, however, took place inside a schoolhouse."

To Samuel, rules were chains, and only fools submitted to them. One day, when he was skipping school, his mother caught him, so she made him paint a fence as punishment. After the first three minutes, Samuel had had enough. He began to moan and groan, carelessly slapping the paint on the fence. Suddenly, he spotted some of his classmates strolling toward him. He had an idea. He stopped groaning and began to act as though he were enjoying himself tremendously. Just as he expected, his classmates fell for the trick. They all wanted a chance to paint the fence, even offering Samuel gifts for a turn with the brush. Within two hours, the fence looked like new. Samuel had done almost no work at all, and he had acquired a doorknob, a frog, a caterpillar, and other precious gifts.

Every year, during the summer, Samuel went to stay with his uncle on his farm. This was his one and only escape from school. To him, the farm was paradise. He and his cousins would run around barefooted, racing each other up walnut trees, having water fights in the creek, hunting for birds' nests in the woods, and eating ripe watermelons in the fields.

ANDREA
DI

Although all sorts of adventures could be had at the farm, the most fun could be had listening to Uncle Daniel's ghost stories. Uncle Daniel was a slave, and in the evenings, the children would gather in his room to hear another story. As soon as Uncle Daniel would intone, "Once upon a time," a cold shiver of fear would snake down Samuel's spine. He wanted to block his ears, but he wanted to listen more. His favorite story was "The Golden Arm," a tale about a thief who stole the golden arm of a ghost.

"Who . . . stole . . . my . . . golden . . . arm?" Uncle Daniel would ask in a ghostly voice as he reached out his hand and pretended to grab one of the children. They were so scared they could hardly breathe or move their heads. They were terrified that if they looked around, they would see the ghost standing behind them. Samuel never forgot Uncle Daniel's amazing talent for storytelling. From the old slave, Samuel learned how much pleasure stories could give.

"I can feel the thumping rain upon my head of hickory nuts and walnuts, when we were out in the frosty dawn to scramble with the pigs. . . . I know the stain of blackberries, and how pretty it is."

When Samuel was eleven, his father died of pneumonia. The family had little money, so Samuel had to leave school and go to work. He began working as an apprentice printer for a local newspaper. His job was to set the type. This meant finding the right pieces of lead type and setting them correctly in trays, ready for printing.

He didn't get paid for his work. Instead, he was given food and a place to sleep, which made things easier for his family. His boss was mean to him. Samuel had to sleep on the floor of his house. The food they fed him was poor,

and there was never enough. When his stomach growled with hunger, he would sneak into the kitchen in the middle of the night to steal a tomato or onion to eat. In spite of these hardships, Samuel had a chance to observe the newspapermen and read what they wrote. This gave him his first experience with newspaper work. Although he didn't know it at the time, he, too, would one day make his living by writing.

One morning on his way to work, the wind blew a small piece of paper across Samuel's path. Curious, he stopped to pick it up. It was a page from the biography of Joan of Arc. Samuel was fascinated by what he read. Joan of Arc was so courageous and noble. History at school had never captured his interest the way this story did. For the first time in his life, he felt books could offer as much excitement as adventure. He began to read historical stories. Soon, the boy who hated school became an avid book-lover.

When Samuel's older brother, Orion, began his own small newspaper, Samuel went to work for him, setting type and occasionally writing short articles. But the newspaper wasn't very successful. So when his rather conservative brother went away on business, Samuel took the opportunity to try to increase the newspaper's circulation by writing humorous sketches for it. One sketch was about the brokenhearted editor of a rival newspaper, who tried to drown himself in the river but had to give up because the water wasn't deep enough. He illustrated this with a cartoon of the editor pacing up and down the riverbank, testing the depth of the water with a stick.

Because of Samuel's funny sketches, the paper's circulation began to grow. But when Orion came home and saw what his brother had done, he was furious. He disapproved of Samuel's humorous style. The paper continued to do badly until it finally had to shut down, but Samuel had discovered his talent.

In the years that followed, Samuel moved from newspaper to newspaper, setting type. It seemed this would be his career for the rest of his life, until the day when he found a $50 bill in the road. He decided to use it to go to South America. He had always wanted to go there. Even though he didn't know how far away it was, Samuel was sure that $50 was a start.

When Samuel returned to the Mississippi to begin his journey, his childhood dream of working on a steamboat quickly made him give up his idea of South America. He started going out without a hat, so the sun would turn him brown and make him look like an experienced sailor. Whenever he could get on the bridge of a steamboat, he would beg the pilot for a chance to hold the wheel. At first, the pilots refused, but finally one gave in and agreed to let him steer for five minutes. Holding the wheel, Samuel felt like a king. Gliding down the Mississippi on a steamboat seemed like a life of freedom.

A pilot's life, he thought, was as free as the wind. To the boy who hated the rules and regulations of school, being a riverboat pilot was the most wonderful thing he could imagine.

For the sum of $500, Samuel was taken on as an apprentice pilot. He carried a pen and notebook with him at all times, recording in it everything the pilot taught him. He also wrote down the special terms used by the crew and his own

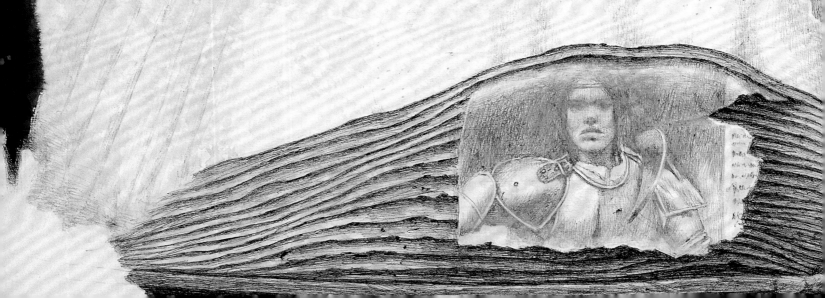

ANDREA
DI
GENNARO

observations of the river. He was taught to remember every reef, sandbank, and island along the river and to watch the current for signs of dangers underneath or ahead.

The Mississippi River played a very important role in Samuel's life. It even gave him the name he later adopted as a writer, Mark Twain. This name meant a lot to Samuel because it was a term for the depth of the river. The river boatmen would use a rope with a lead weight on the end to test the river's depth. If the water was less than two fathoms (12 feet) deep, the boatmen would call out, "Mark twain," meaning it wasn't safe for the boat to continue.

"A pilot, in those days, was the only unfettered and entirely independent human being that lived on earth. Kings are but the hampered servants of parliament. . . . In truth, every man, woman, and child has a master, but . . . the Mississippi pilot had none."

After several years working on the Mississippi, Samuel finally became a pilot. But soon, the Civil War disrupted shipping, and Samuel had to return home. In Hannibal, his friends supported the South, but Samuel wanted to see the slaves freed. He decided to enlist in the army. On his way to camp, however, he passed the perfect spot to swim and fish. As he dropped his pack and tore off his uniform, his enthusiasm for fighting vanished. After enjoying himself, he headed back home.

After the Civil War, Samuel went with his brother Orion to Nevada. Excited about setting off for the unknown, he was full of expectations about what he would find. He thought this was his chance to make his fortune.

Very soon, Samuel and a friend named John Kinney found a nice piece of woodland they intended to claim for themselves, as the law allowed. Unfortunately, their happiness came to a quick end. One evening, when they lit a fire to cook their meal, sparks leaped from the blaze and set the dry pine needles on fire. Soon, their entire property was burning. They were lucky to escape with their lives, and their dreams of a fortune went up in smoke.

Samuel's next venture was silver mining. This time, he teamed up with an engineer named Calvin Higbie. They slept on the ground and wore the same filthy clothes day after day, digging until the air was thick with dust. Finally, at the end of the week, they found silver. By law, as long as they filed a claim within ten days, all the silver they found would be theirs.

But then Calvin Higbie was called away to investigate a mine in California, and Samuel was called away by his brother. They left notes for each other, each asking the other to take care of the claim. Unfortunately, neither of them received the other's message. When they returned to the mine, they found that instead of being millionaires, their silver had been claimed by someone else. Samuel lost another fortune.

Samuel wrote about his lost fortunes and sent the story to a newspaper. Not only was the story published, but also Samuel was hired as a reporter. He leapt at the chance. At the time, he had only two dollars in his pocket.

Although Samuel had never thought about becoming a writer, working as a reporter had awakened his love for writing. He was a brilliant observer and everything that passed before his eyes was etched in his brain. His brain held a vast bank of images and memories on which he could draw for his stories.

His work was beginning to attract attention, and he started using the name "Mark Twain." But Samuel wasn't really a good journalist. Whenever he felt a story was dull, he would invent a few extra details or stretch the truth. He believed a journalist's main goal was to keep the reader entertained. If the facts weren't interesting the way they were, he felt that it was right to add a few flourishes or whatever it took to liven up the story.

Mark Twain was now writing many humorous sketches. One example was a hoax about a petrified man. The sketch tells of how a mummified human body had been found, sitting in a thoughtful position but stuck to the rock behind it. At an inquest investigating the cause of death, the jury gave the verdict that the man died of prolonged exposure. The judge decided the body shouldn't be blasted from the rock and given a proper burial, so it became a local attraction. Of course, none of this story was true.

Eventually, one of these humorous sketches caught up with Twain. He wrote a story about a charity organization that collected money not to care for soldiers wounded in the Civil War, as it claimed, but to promote marriages between former slaves and white people. The readers were shocked.

ANDREA
DI

In the 1860s, racial intermarriage was unacceptable and never talked about. The storm of anger this story caused frightened Mark Twain so much that he fled to San Francisco.

Disappointed and humbled by this experience, Mark Twain once again was out of work. So he joined the gold rush. In the gold fields, the miners would sit around the fire at night and tell stories to amuse each other. An old miner named Ben Coon told a story about a frog, a frog who could jump farther than any other frog.

Mark Twain liked this story and decided to write it down, just as Ben Coon had told it. He called it "Jim Smiley and His Jumping Frog." The story was published in a New York paper. It was an instant hit, going on to appear in every major magazine in America. Mark Twain had leapt into fame with a frog. He became known as the "Wild Humorist of the Pacific Slope."

Next, Mark Twain was invited to Hawaii to write a series of articles for a magazine on the life and customs of the people. When he arrived, 15 survivors of a shipwreck had just been found after being adrift on the ocean for 43 days. Twain immediately interviewed the men and rushed his report back to a newspaper. This article created a sensation throughout America.

When he returned from Hawaii, a friend persuaded him to give a public lecture. Twain quickly captivated the crowd, for he was an excellent storyteller. He knew just when to pause, exactly how to build a mood, how to make people laugh, and how to create a warm and friendly atmosphere.

Mark Twain was now 30 years old, and his popularity was growing. He toured the country and published a collection of his humorous sketches. For the

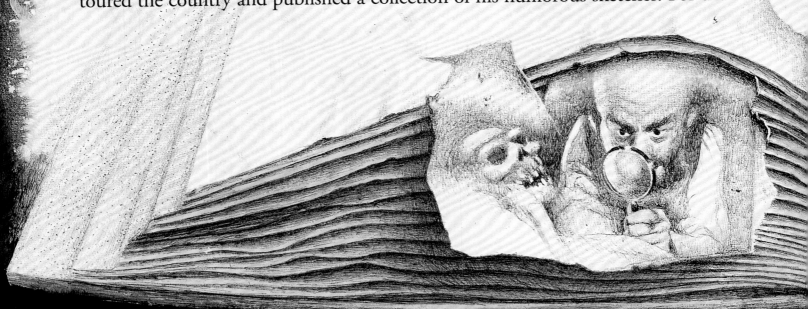

next 20 years, writing and lecturing were his main occupations. He became a best-selling author and a famous lecturer. Like most other successful writers, he wrote best about what he knew. Two of his best-known books are *The Adventures of Tom Sawyer* and *The Adventures of Huckleberry Finn*. Both novels are about the lives of young boys. This isn't surprising, as Twain believed childhood was the most wonderful part of life. He once wrote, "When one writes a novel about grown people, he know exactly where to stop—that is, with marriage; but when he writes of juveniles, he must stop where best he can."

In *The Adventures of Huckleberry Finn*, he wrote about his hometown of Hannibal, renamed St. Petersburg, and many of his childhood experiences, such as skipping school and playing on the Mississippi. In *Tom Sawyer*, he modeled the character of Tom on himself and Tom's friend, Huck, on his own childhood friend, Tom. Aunt Polly was modeled on his mother.

"Writing is an art. The difference between the right word and the almost right word is really a large matter—it's the difference between the lightening bug and the lightening," wrote Mark Twain.

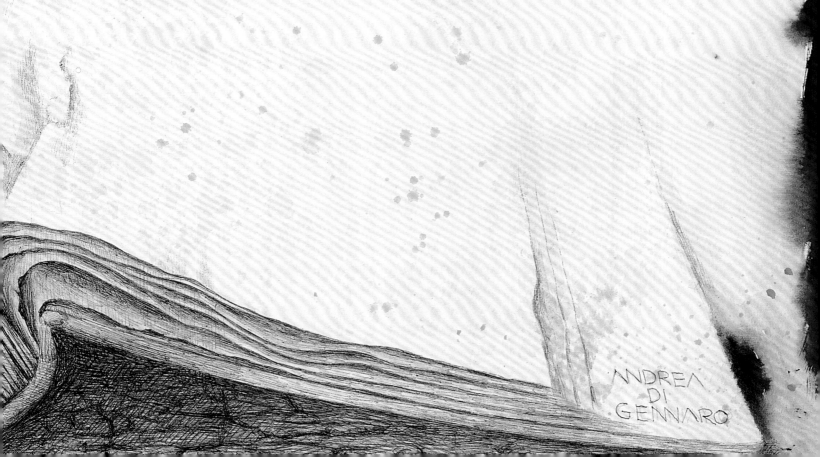

In 1902, Mark Twain returned to his hometown to present the students at his old school with their graduation certificates. He was no longer an adventurous child, but his blue gray eyes sparkled with merriment, and he spoke with the same sense of humor.

In 1907, he was awarded an honorary degree from Oxford University in England, recognizing his contributions to literature. Twain had never even graduated from high school.

In 1910, the year of the return of Halley's Comet, Mark Twain wrote: "My own bottom still tingles from the switchings I received from my teachers. Now I'm handing out diplomas. Life does take some strange turns indeed." And so it was. When Halley's Comet once again crossed the skies above the earth, Samuel Langhorne Clemens quietly took his leave of the world and followed the comet into history. His works remain alive, bringing pleasure to generation after generation of children and adults around the world.

"I have not professionally dealt in truth. Many when they come to die have spent all the truth that was in them, and enter the next world as paupers. I have saved up enough to make an astonishment there."

ANDREA
DI
GENNARO

BIOGRAPHY

Author Anna Carew-Miller is a freelance writer and former teacher, who lives in rural northwestern Connecticut with her husband and daughter. Although she has a Ph.D. in American Literature and has done extensive research and writing on literary topics, more recently, Anna has written books for younger readers, including reference books and middle reader mysteries.